Two Minute SQL Server Stumpers

Vol. 3

Brought to you by the staff at
SQLServerCentral.com

Thanks to the following for contributing questions:

Mike Ngong
Robert Marda
Jonathan Shyman

Central Publishing Group
P.O. Box 9510
Fleming Island, FL 32006

Copyright Notice

Disclaimer

Trademarks

Forward

Why Two Minute Questions?

When I was a kid, I used to order these Scholastic mysteries from the school. They were these little, thin paperbacks, like 50-60 or so pages, much like what you're holding now, that had a short mystery written on a page. Usually they consisted of some story and then a question. How did someone get killed? Where did the murder weapon go? Something like that. You then turned the page to find out the answer after thinking about it for a minute.

We're back with Volume 2 and once again, that's what we're trying to build here, but instead of some mystery, it's a quiz type format of SQL Server questions and answers, culled from the annals of our very popular Question Of The Day on the SQLServerCentral.com website. These are a collection of questions from the past that we put together to help you study for an exam, learn a bit more about SQL Server, pass the time, etc. But they're mostly collected for...

The INTERVIEW.

You're looking for a new job, you've posted your resume, worked on cover letters, and finally landed an interview. Now you want to be sure that you look your best; that you can answer what's thrown at you.

I can't promise that anyone will ask you any of these questions, but you never know. Maybe some managers that are interviewing will grab a copy of the book and start asking questions out of it. But it will help you prepare, give you some hands on experience, challenge you in a variety of ways about the different aspects of SQL Server. Some of the questions are arcane, some very common, but you'll learn something and the wide range of questions will help you get your mind agile and ready for some quick thinking.

So read on, in order, randomly, just start going through them, but do yourself a favor and think about each before turning the page. Challenge yourself and see how well you do.

Thanks for your support and be sure to visit us online.

Steve Jones
SQLServerCentral.com

Answer:

3. DBCC SQLPERF (LOGSPACE)
The DBCC command DBCC SQLPERF with the parameter of LOGSPACE will show you the database name, the size of the log in MB and the percent that is being used of the log.
Ref: DBCC SQLPERF -
http://msdn.microsoft.com/library/default.asp?url=/library/en-us/tsqlref/ts_dbcc_5vja.asp

Question 2 - Administration

You are trying to automate your monitoring and you wish to alert yourself if a give database's log file fills up. Which of the following T-SQL statements would let you see how much transaction log space you have allocated to each database and how much of that is actually being used?

Choose one of the answers below:

1. SP_HELP
2. SP_SPACEUSED
3. DBCC SQLPERF (LOGSPACE)
4. None of the above
5. All the above will work

Answer:

4. SQL Server is set to Windows Only Authentication
During installation, SQL Server will ask you what authentication type you would like to setup for the server, SQL Server and Windows or Windows Only. The default option is Windows Only. If you specify this option, then you will be unable to connect to the SQL Server with SQL Server authentication. You would receive this error if you connected to SQL Server for sa for example.

Question 1 - Administration

What is the most likely reason for receiving the following error when signing in with the sa account?
Login failed- User: Reason: Not defined as a valid user of a trusted SQL Server connection.

Choose one of the answers below:

1. The account your application is using doesn't have the appropriate SQL Server permissions.
2. Your domain account does not have log on locally rights.
3. SQL Server is set to Mixed Authentication mode.
4. SQL Server is set to Windows Only Authentication
5. SQL Server's master database is corrupt

Question 3 - Administration

You are trying to monitor information about the procedure cache and track the information historically. To do this, you've created the following table:

CREATE TABLE PROCCACHE (numprocbuffs int, numprocbuffsused int, numprocbuffsactive int, proccachesize int, proccacheused int, proccacheactive int)
and you hope to run DBCC PROCCACHE on a periodic basis and load the results into the table. What syntax could best accomplish your task? Choose one of the answers below:

1. INSERT INTO PROCCACHE (numprocbuffs, numprocbuffsused, numprocbuffsactive,
proccachesize, proccacheused, proccacheactive)
VALUES(EXECUTE DBCC PROCCACHE)
2. INSERT INTO PROCCACHE (numprocbuffs, numprocbuffsused, numprocbuffsactive,
proccachesize, proccacheused, proccacheactive)
EXECUTE 'DBCC PROCCACHE'
3. INSERT INTO PROCCACHE (numprocbuffs, numprocbuffsused, numprocbuffsactive,
proccachesize, proccacheused, proccacheactive)
EXECUTE (DBCC PROCCACHE)
4. INSERT INTO PROCCACHE (numprocbuffs, numprocbuffsused, numprocbuffsactive,
proccachesize, proccacheused, proccacheactive)
EXECUTE ('DBCC PROCCACHE')
5. None of the above

Answer:

4. INSERT INTO PROCCACHE (numprocbuffs, numprocbuffsused, numprocbuffsactive,
proccachesize, proccacheused, proccacheactive)
EXECUTE ('DBCC PROCCACHE')
DBCC PROCCACHE displays information in a table format about the procedure cache. To load the results of a DBCC statement into a table, you must issue the EXECUTE statement and place the statement in single quotes.
Ref: DBCC PROCCACHE -
http://msdn.microsoft.com/library/default.asp?url=/library/en-us/tsqlref/ts_dbcc_61d1.asp

Question 4 - Administration

You are a DBA who supports a development group who uses DCOM calls to the SQL Server Distributed Transaction Coordinator (MSDTC) often. The application works great in development but when you deploy into production, which is in a protected firewall environment, the areas of the application that use MSDTC fail. You suspect it is a firewall problem. What ports should you open in the firewall to make the application work?

Choose one of the answers below:

1. Open port 1433 bi-directionally between servers
2. Port 134 bi-directionally between servers
3. MSDTC sets the port at install. You can see what port is being used in Enterprise Manager under Support Services | Distributed Transaction Coordinator | Properties
4. MSDTC uses random ports. You will need to modify the registry on the server making the connection to narrow down what ports it uses and open the firewall to those ports.
5. MSDTC uses random ports. You will need to modify the registry on the server where MSDTC is on to narrow down what ports it uses and open the firewall to those ports.
6. MSDTC uses random ports. You will need to modify the registry on both servers to narrow down what ports it uses and open the firewall to those ports.

Answer:

6. MSDTC uses random ports. You will need to modify the registry on both servers to narrow down what ports it uses and open the firewall to those ports.
DTC uses Remote Procedure Call (RPC) dynamic port allocation. By default, RPC dynamic port allocation randomly selects port numbers above 1024. By modifying the registry, you can control which ports RPC dynamically allocates for incoming communication. You can then configure your firewall to confine incoming external communication to only those ports and port 135 (the RPC Endpoint Mapper port). For more information on configuring MSDTC for a firewall, see http://support.microsoft.com/default.aspx?scid=kb;EN-US;250367.

Question 5 - Administration

You are a DBA who is trying to attach to a MDF and LDF file that are on the network temporarily. When you try to do this though, you receive an error 5110 from SQL Server.
"File filename.mdf is on a network device not supported for database files."

How can you accomplish this task?
Contributed Lina
Choose one of the answers below:

1. It is impossible
2. Start SQL Server in a single user mode
3. Start SQL Server in minimal mode
4. Turn on trace flag 1807
5. Turn on trace flage 3608

Answer:

4. Turn on trace flag 1807

To use database file on network device It's required a trace flag (1807) to be turned on. Microsoft does not recommend that you do this however since it's difficult to guarantee IO to a network device.

Question 6 - Administration

You installed SQL Server on the C drive when you first built your SQL Server and now wish to move the tempdb database since it's filling up your drive. You first find out some key information by running:

```
use tempdb
go
sp_helpfile
go
```

This tells you that the file is currently logically named tempdev and templog. Physically it is stored at C:\Sql_data\tempdb.mdf and C:\Sql_data\templog.ldf. How do you accomplish the task of moving the tempdb to the E drive into a directory called SQL_Data. Note: The assumption is that you will stop and start SQL Server after you perform this action.

Choose one of the answers below:

1. Alter database tempdb modify file (name = tempdev, source = 'C:\Sql_data\tempdb.mdf' destination='E:\Sql_data\tempdb.mdf')
go
Alter database tempdb modify file (name = templog, source = 'C:\Sql_data\templog.ldf' destination='E:\Sql_data\templog.ldf')
go

2. Alter database tempdb modify file (name = tempdev, filename = 'E:\Sql_data\tempdb.mdf')
go
Alter database tempdb modify file (name = templog, filename = 'E:\Sql_data\templog.ldf')

3. Right-click on the tempdb database, select Properties. Change the location in the Data File and Transaction Log File tabs.
4. Right-click on the tempdb database, select Properties. Add a new file in the new location. Stop and start SQL Server. Then remove the old file.
5. Detach and attach the tempdb files.
6. Backup and restore the tempdb files.

Answer:

2.

```
use master
go
Alter database tempdb modify file (name = tenpdev,
filename = 'E:\Sql_data\tempdb.mdf')
go
Alter database tempdb modify file (name = tenplog,
filename = 'E:\Sql_data\templog.ldf')
go
```

Determine the logical file names for the **tempdb** database by using **sp_helpfile** as follows:

```
sp_helpfile
go
```

The logical name for each file is contained in the **name** column. This example uses the default file names of **tempdev** and **templog**. Use the ALTER DATABASE statement, specifying the logical file name as follows:

```
use master
go
Alter database tempdb modify file (name = tenpdev,
filename = 'E:\Sqldata\tempdb.mdf')
go
Alter database tempdb modify file (name = tenplog,
filename = 'E:\Sqldata\templog.ldf')
go
```

You should receive the following messages confirming the change:
File 'tempdev' modified in sysaltfiles. Delete old file after restarting SQL Server.

File 'templog' modified in sysaltfiles. Delete old file after restarting SQL Server.
Using **sp_helpfile** in **tempdb** will not confirm these changes until you restart SQL Server.
Stop and restart SQL Server.
Ref: Moving SQL Server databases to a new location with Detach/Attach - http://support.microsoft.com/default.aspx?scid=kb;en-us;224071&Product=sql2k

Question 7 - Administration

You have the following objects in one SQL Server 2000 database:

```
CREATE TABLE DebugMe (RecordNumber int NOT NULL
IDENTITY (1,1), MyComments varchar(50))
ALTER TABLE DebugMe ADD CONSTRAINT cc_MyComments
CHECK (MyComments LIKE '[a-z]%')
CREATE UNIQUE INDEX IX_MyComments ON DebugMe
(MyComments) WITH FILLFACTOR = 100 ON [PRIMARY]
CREATE TRIGGER IAlwaysFire ON DebugMe FOR INSERT
AS
UPDATE m SET MyComments = i.MyComments + 'tr'
FROM DebugMe m LEFT JOIN inserted i ON i.RecordNumber
= m.RecordNumber
CREATE PROCEDURE RunMe (@MyComments varchar(20) =
'none')
AS
IF LEFT(@MyComments, 1) < 't'
   SET @MyComments = 'changed'
INSERT INTO DebugMe (MyComments) VALUES (@MyComments)
GO
You execute in Query Analyzer this code:
EXEC RunMe @MyComments = 'one'
EXEC RunMe @MyComments = 'two'
EXEC RunMe @MyComments = 'three'
In the results window you see this:
(1 row(s) affected)
(1 row(s) affected)
(2 row(s) affected)
(1 row(s) affected)
Server: Msg 2601, Level 14, State 3, Procedure
IAlwaysFire, Line 6
Cannot insert duplicate key row in object 'DebugMe'
with unique index 'IX_MyComments'.
The statement has been terminated.
```

Why did you get this error when you used 3 different values for @MyComments? Choose one of the answers below:

1. The stored procedure did not use the values you sent in. It replaced them all with the word changed.
2. The trigger is updating all previous values for the column MyComments with NULL.
3. The check constraint caused the unique index to only consider the first character of each inserted value.
4. This is a known bug in SQL Server 2000 and will be resolved with the next service pack.

Answer:

2. The trigger is updating all previous values for the column MyComments with NULL.
If you look closely you will notice that the trigger is updating the column MyComments with the value from the inserted table. Since the SP RunMe only adds one row each time it is run there will not be more than one row in the inserted table. When you execute the second SP call the trigger updates the first row with a NULL value. When you execute the third SP call the trigger tries to update the second row with NULL and that update would violate the unique index and so you get the error.

Question 8 - Administration

A DBA comes to you puzzled about the size of the database. He had run sp_spaceused to determine how much space the database was using and it had returned an unexpected result. The space was substantially off. What is the most likely solution to fix this (assuming you were in the db when you do this for the T-SQL statement)?

Choose one of the answers below:

1. Stop and start SQL Server
2. Reboot the server
3. Run DBCC UPDATECACHE
4. Run DBCC UPDATEUSAGE (0)
5. Run DBCC CHECKDB

Answer:

4. Run DBCC UPDATEUSAGE (0)
DBCC UPDATEUSAGE reports and corrects inaccuracies in the sysindexes table, which may result in incorrect space usage reports by the sp_spaceused system stored procedure.
Ref: DBCC UPDATEUSAGE -
http://msdn.microsoft.com/library/default.asp?url=/library/en-us/tsqlref/ts_dbcc_24rp.asp

Question 9 - Administration

You are a SQL Server DBA and you suspect the server doesn't have enough RAM and is paging. What is the easiest method to determine how much paging is occuring on your system to see if you need more RAM? Note: We are assuming you have a baseline to compare against.

Choose one of the answers below:

1. In Performance Monitor's System Object : Avg. Disk Queue Length
2. In Performance Monitor's Memory Object : Pages/Sec
3. In Performance Monitor's System Object : Process Object : % Processor Time
4. Right-click on My Computer, go to the Advanced tab and select Settings under Performance.
5. In Profiler under the PageFile object

Answer:

2. In Performance Monitor's Memory Object : Pages/Sec
For more counter information, see http://www.sqlservercentral.com/columnists/sjones/performancemonitoringbasiccounters.asp. This is a counter that cannot really be measured independent of a system. In other words, I can't tell you that 1,000 pages/sec is a high or low value. It really depends on your system. So it's a relative counter, one that you want to watch so you can tell if things are changing. You make a change and see if the counter goes up or down. In general, adding memory (or allocating more to SQL) should lower this counter, but you have to be careful.
Page Faults/sec is another counter that is recommended by many people. They both can help you to view whether or not memory is an issue. If you allocated too much memory to SQL and starved the OS, this could go up. Again, it depends on your system, so get a baseline of this and then watch it as you make changes.

Question 10 - Administration

You have setup SQL Server Agents alerts to notify you when certain performance measures are reached. What is one thing to keep in mind when creating alerts like this?

Choose one of the answers below:

1. The table that holds the performance info is only updated once every hour
2. The table that holds the performance info is only updated once every 30 minutes
3. Only the first 99 databases are included in the table that holds the performance info
4. Only the first 500 databaes are included in the table that holds the performance info
5. The sp_add_alert stored procedure can't setup alerts of this sort
6. None of the above are true

Answer:

3. Only the first 99 databases are included in the table that holds the performance info

Performance condition alerts are only available for the first 99 databases. Any databases created after the first 99 databases will not be included in the sysperfinfo system table, and using the sp_add_alert procedure will return an error.

Ref: BUG: SQLServer:Databases Performance Counters Limited to First 99 Databases in Windows System Monitor - http://support.microsoft.com/default.aspx?scid=kb;en-us;330088

Question 11 - Administration

You have a small shopping cart application and periodically want to alter the prices for various items in the database. You generate a script for changes to individual line items, but you want to be sure that no one purchases an item while the script runs since there will be some strange prices between items. You decide that you want to force SQL Server to perform table locking for the duration of your script on the LineItems table. There is only one index on LineItems, LineItems.ItemNo
Choose one of the answers below:

1. exec sp_changetablelock [dbo.LineItems.ItemNo], 'table_level'
2. exec sp_indexoption 'LineItems.ItemNo', 'allowtablelocks', 'true'
3. EXEC sp_indexoption 'LineItems.ItemNo', 'disallowpagelocks', TRUE
EXEC sp_indexoption 'LineItems.ItemNo', 'disallowrowlocks', TRUE
4. None of the above, you cannot specify force SQL Server to use a table lock.

Answer:

3. EXEC sp_indexoption 'LineItems.ItemNo', 'disallowpagelocks', TRUE
EXEC sp_indexoption 'LineItems.ItemNo', 'disallowrowlocks', TRUE
SQL Server chooses whether to use row, page, or table locks automatically. You can set a particular table to use a different locking strategy with *sp_indexoption*. You can allow or disallow both row and page level locks to force SQL Server to choose one or more of the remaining three.
Ref: http://msdn.microsoft.com/library/default.asp?url=/library/en-us/tsqlref/ts_sp_ia-iz_5t7y.asp

Question 12 - Administration

What's the difference between user_name() and suser_sname()?
Choose one of the answers below:

1. User_name() returns the name of the logged in user while suser_sname() returns the name of the network user.
2. There is no difference.
3. User_name() returns the name of the current user in the database while suser_sname() returns the network user.
4. User_name() returns the name of the current user in the database while suser_sname() returns the server login user.

Answer:

4. User_name() returns the name of the current user in the database while suser_sname() returns the server login user.
The user_name() command returns the current database user, which could be altered with setuser. suser_sname() returns the login name used to log into the SQL Server.

Question 13 - Administration

What is the difference between using the NO_LOG and TRUNCATE_ONLY options when backing up a transaction log in SQL Server 2000?
Choose one of the answers below:

1. The NO_LOG option will perform a backup of the transaction log to a file before truncating the log while the TRUNCATE_ONLY merely truncates the log.
2. The TRUNCATE_ONLY option will perform a backup of the transaction log to a file before truncating the log while the NO_LOG merely truncates the log.
3. The NO_LOG option will truncate the active portion of the log without making an entry into the log. The TRUNCATE_ONLY option truncates the log, but makes an entry in the log.
4. There is no difference.

Answer:

4. There is no difference.
There is no difference between these options. They are synonyms.
Ref: Backup - http://msdn.microsoft.com/library/default.asp?url=/library/en-us/tsqlref/ts_ba-bz_35ww.asp.

Question 14 - Administration

You run a backup of your SQL Server 2000 Sales database to the same file with a different backup set each night. The backup sets are set to expire after eight days and you have room on disk (by your estimate) for 12 days worth of backups to this file.
Which option for the backup command would get you into trouble on the 13th day? Assume only one of these options is specified.
Choose one of the answers below:

1. NOSKIP
2. NOEXPIRE
3. SKIP
4. NOUNLOAD

Answer:

3. SKIP
The SKIP option disables the checking for expired backup sets. If you include this option, then you will not expire any backup sets and you will run out of disk space. NOSKIP would not check the backup dates and NOUNLOAD deals with having the tape eject on tape drives. NOEXPIRE is not a valid option.

Ref: BACKUP - http://msdn.microsoft.com/library/default.asp?url=/library/en-us/tsqlref/ts_ba-bz_35ww.asp

Question 15 - Administration

A developer reboots his workstation and his personal edition of SQL Server fails to start. He shows you the following entry in the error log: 2001-11-14 15:49:14.12 server SuperSocket Info: Bind failed on TCP port 1433.

What is the likely cause of this?
Choose one of the answers below:

1. Another application is listening on this port.
2. The SQL Server is configured for another port.
3. The network adapter needs to be reseated in the machine.
4. The SQL Server is configured for TCP/IP and the computer is not running this protocol.

Answer:

1. Another application is listening on this port.
This is described in KB article 293107 and usually occurs when another application has already bound to this port.

Question 16 - Administration

A database's syscolumns table contains one record for every column in:

Choose one of the answers below:

1. every table
2. every table and every view
3. every table, every view and every stored procedure parameter list
4. every table, every view, every stored procedure parameter list and every UDF parameter.

Answer:

4. every table, every view, every stored procedure parameter list and every UDF parameter.

BOL is incorrect in not mentioning UDFs. There is a row for each of these items : table, view, stored procedure, stored procedure parameter (each one), UDF, UDF parameter (each one).

Ref: syscolumns - http://msdn.microsoft.com/library/default.asp?url=/library/en-us/tsqlref/ts_sys-c_5mur.asp

Question 17 - Administration

AWE allows SQL Server to address how much memory on SQL Server 2000 (32 bit) Enterprise Edition? (The max on any edition of Windows) Choose one of the answers below:

1. 32GB
2. 8GB
3. 64GB
4. 256GB

Answer:

3. 64GB
64GB of RAM is addressable using AWE on W2K Data Center.
Ref: Using AWE Memory on Windows 2000 - http://msdn.microsoft.com/library/default.asp?url=/library/en-us/architec/8_ar_sa_6b3k.asp

Question 18 - Administration

Which edition of SQL Server 2000 below can support the largest database?
Choose one of the answers below:

1. SQL Server 2000 Standard Edition
2. SQL Server 2000 Enterprise Edition
3. SQL Server 2000 Enterprise Edition (64-bit)
4. They all support the same size database.
5. SQL Server 2000 Developer Edition

Answer:

4. They all support the same size database.
According to
http://www.microsoft.com/sql/evaluation/overview/default.asp, all three editions support the same maximum database size.

Question 19 - Administration

Is it possible to programmatically detect a blocked connection without querying the system tables directly?

Choose one of the answers below:

1. Yes
2. No, you must query the system tables to find blocks in your program.

Answer:

1. Yes
You can insert the results of sp_who2 into a table and then query for any entries in the "blkby" column.

Question 20 - Administration

Why do the sp_depends procedure and the Display Dependencies in Enterprise Manager sometimes show different results?

Choose one of the answers below:

1. Your database is corrupt.
2. The Enterprise Manager display uses an undocumented stored procedure sp_MSdependencies, which operates differently than sp_depends.
3. There are bugs in the Enterprise Manager display.
4. sp_depends only shows dependencies on tables owned by dbo. Enterprise Manager shows all table dependencies.

Answer:

2. The Enterprise Manager display uses an undocumented stored procedure sp_MSdependencies, which operates differently than sp_depends.
Enterprise manager calls the undocumented stored procedure sp_msDependnecies, which moves through multiple levels and gets more information than sp_depends.

Ref: Displaying Dependencies - http://www.microsoft.com/sql/techinfo/tips/development/displayingdependencies.asp.

Question 21 - Administration

What does this return?

EXEC master..xp_msver N'ProcessorCount',N'ProcessorType'

Choose one of the answers below:

1. It returns the Intel CPU serial number and speed
2. It returns the number of CPUs count and the type of processor.
3. It returns the number of processors and the affinity mask
4. It returns the number of processors and the processor speed.

Answer:

2. It returns the number of CPUs count and the type of processor. This returns the processor count and the processor family, 586, 686, etc.

Ref: xp_msver - http://msdn.microsoft.com/library/default.asp?url=/library/en-us/tsqlref/ts_xp_aa-sz_0o4y.asp.

Question 22 - Administration

Where can I find all the ports on which my SQL Server 2000 server is listenting?

Choose one of the answers below:

1. Enterprise Manager, SQL Server, Properties, Network Configuration, TCP/IP, Properties.
2. My Computer, Manage, Services, MSSQLServer, Properties, Network Tab.
3. My Computer, Manage, Services, MSSQLServer, Properties, parameter passed into startup command.
4. The SQL Server error log.

Answer:

4. The SQL Server error log.
In the SQL Server error log, all the ports that SQL Server is listening on when it starts are listed. The Server Network Utility will also show this.

Question 23 - Administration

How can you identify automatically created statistics in the sysindexes table in SQL Server 2000?

Choose one of the answers below:

1. Select an index, right click, properties, look for the "System Generated" checkbox.
2. Indexes that are named _sys_wa in sysindexes are automatically created.
3. sp_helpstatistics gives you all automatically created indexes.
4. Indexes that are named _WA_Sys in sysindexes are automatically created.

Answer:

4. Indexes that are named _WA_Sys in sysindexes are automatically created.

The indexes in sysindexes with a prefix of _WA_Sys are statistical indexes that SQL Server automatically creates.

Question 24 - Administration

I recently changed the SQL Server 2000 default instant security mode from mixed to Windows only. However I had removed the BUILTIN/Adminstrators group from the sysadmin group. Now I cannot log in as a system admin. How can I get back in to my server? I know the sa password.

Choose one of the answers below:

1. Change the following key to have a value of 2: HKEY_LOCAL_MACHINE\SOFTWARE\MicrosoftMicrosoftSQLServer\\MSSQLServer\LoginMode
2. Change the following key to have a value of 2:HKLM\Software\Microsoft\MSSqlserver\MSSqlServer\LoginMode
3. Just log in with the sa account and password. Use isqlw.exe with the -A switch.
4. Domain administrators can still login as sysadmins. Use one of those accounts.

Answer:

2. Change the following key to have a value of 2:HKLM\Software\Microsoft\MSSqlserver\MSSqlServer\LoginMode This key determines the security mode for SQL Server 2000. A 2 indicates mixed mode. This key is referenced in Microsoft Knowledge Base Article - 285097. If you set this to mixed mode, you can log in with the sa account and then add additional accounts as needed.

Question 25 - Administration

In SQL Server 2000's Query Analyzer, by right clicking on a table, you cannot generate a script for which of the following items for a table.

Choose one of the answers below:

1. Index
2. Insert
3. Update
4. Create
5. Delete
6. Drop

Answer:

1. Index
You cannot generate an index script. This option is not available in the SQL 2000 query analyzer tool. When you right click a table, you will have the following scripting options:

- Create
- Drop
- Select
- Insert
- Update
- Delete

Question 26 - Administration

What is the Maximum number of tables and columns that SQL Server 2000 Enterprise edition can support in a single database?

Choose one of the answers below:

1. One Billion tables with 512 columns per table
2. Two Billion tables with 512 columns per table
3. One Billion tables with 1024 columns per table
4. Two Billion tables with 1024 columns per table

Answer:

4. Two Billion tables with 1024 columns per table
SQL Server can have as many as two billion tables per database and 1,024 columns per table.
Reference: SQL Server Maximum Capacity Specifications - http://msdn.microsoft.com/library/default.asp?url=/library/en-us/architec/8_ar_ts_8dbn.asp

Question 27 - Administration

What does ACID stand for?

Choose one of the answers below:

1. Atomicity Consistency Integrity Dependable
2. Atomicity Consistency Isolation Durability
3. Atomicity Completeness Isolation Durability
4. Atomicity Completeness Integrity Durability

Answer:

2. Atomicity Consistency Isolation Durability
In the context of database transactions, ACID is an acronym for Atomic, Consistent, Isolation, and Durable. Transactions provide a simple model of success or failure. A transaction either commits (i.e. all its actions happen), or it aborts (i.e. all its actions are undone). This all-or-nothing quality makes for a simple programming model.

Question 28 - Administration

Which of the following is equivalent to executing "sp_who" on SQL Server 2000?
contributed by Necrossomus

Choose one of the answers below:

1.

```
Select Spid,Ecid,Sysprocesses.
Status,Loginame,Hostname,
      Sysprocesses.Blocked ,dbname,cmd,Program_Name
      From Syslogins
      Left join Sysprocesses On Syslogins.Sid =
Sysprocesses.Sid
      Right join Sysdatabases On Sysprocesses.Dbid =
Sysdatabases.Dbid
      Order by Spid
```

2.

```
Select Spid,Ecid,Sysprocesses.
Status,Loginame,Hostname,
      Sysprocesses.Blocked ,dbname,cmd,Program_Name
      From Syslogins
      join Sysprocesses On Syslogins.Sid =
Sysprocesses.Sid
      join Sysdatabases On Sysprocesses.Dbid =
Sysdatabases.Dbid
      Order by Spid
```

3.

```
select spid, ecid, status, loginame=rtrim(loginame),
hostname, blk=convert(char(5),blocked)
     , dbname = case
      when dbid = 0 then null
      when dbid <> 0 then db_name(dbid)
     end
     ,cmd
  from  master.dbo.sysprocesses
  Order by Spid
```

4.

```
Select Spid,Ecid,Sysprocesses.
Status,Loginame,Hostname,
```

```
      Sysprocesses.Blocked ,dbname,cmd,Program_Name
      From Syslogins
      Right join Sysprocesses On Syslogins.Sid =
Sysprocesses.Sid
      Right join Sysdatabases On Sysprocesses.Dbid =
Sysdatabases.Dbid
      Order by Spid
```

Answer:

3.

```
select spid, ecid, status, loginame=rtrim(loginame),
hostname, blk=convert(char(5),blocked)
    , dbname = case
     when dbid = 0 then null
     when dbid <> 0 then db_name(dbid)
    end
    ,cmd
  from  master.dbo.sysprocesses
  Order by Spid
```

The right and left join queries will not return the same results as sp_who will. Answer C is the one that mimics the rows from sp_who.

Question 29 - Administration

What is the correct order to enable Full text indexing in the Northwind database for the Categories table?
contributed by Necrossomus

Choose one of the answers below:

1.
```
Use Northwind
Exec sp_fulltext_database 'Enable'
Go
Exec sp_fulltext_catalog 'Cat_Categories', 'Create'
Go
Exec sp_fulltext_table 'Categories','Create',
'Cat_Categories','PK_Categories'
Go
Exec sp_fulltext_table 'Categories',  'Activate'
Go
Exec sp_fulltext_column
'Categories','Description','Add'
Go
Exec sp_fulltext_catalog 'Cat_Categories',
'Start_Full'
```

2.
```
Use Northwind
Exec sp_fulltext_database 'Enable'
Go
Exec sp_fulltext_catalog 'Cat_Categories', 'Create'
Go
Exec sp_fulltext_table 'Categories','Create',
'Cat_Categories','PK_Categories'
Go
Exec sp_fulltext_column
'Categories','Description','Add'
Go
Exec sp_fulltext_table 'Categories',  'Activate'
Go
Exec sp_fulltext_catalog 'Cat_Categories',
'Start_Full'
```

3.
```
Use Northwind
Exec sp_fulltext_database 'Enable'
Go
```

```
Exec sp_fulltext_table 'Categories','Create',
'Cat_Categories','PK_Categories'
Go
Exec sp_fulltext_catalog 'Cat_Categories', 'Create'
Go
Exec sp_fulltext_column
'Categories','Description','Add'
Go
Exec sp_fulltext_table 'Categories',  'Activate'
Go
Exec sp_fulltext_catalog 'Cat_Categories',
'Start_Full'
```

4.

```
Use Northwind
Exec sp_fulltext_database 'Enable'
Go
Exec sp_fulltext_table 'Categories','Create',
'Cat_Categories','PK_Categories'
Go
Exec sp_fulltext_catalog 'Cat_Categories', 'Create'
Go
```

Answer:

2.

```
Use Northwind
Exec sp_fulltext_database 'Enable'
Go
Exec sp_fulltext_catalog 'Cat_Categories', 'Create'
Go
Exec sp_fulltext_table 'Categories','Create',
'Cat_Categories','PK_Categories'
Go
Exec sp_fulltext_column
'Categories','Description','Add'
Go
Exec sp_fulltext_table 'Categories',  'Activate'
Go
Exec sp_fulltext_catalog 'Cat_Categories',
'Start_Full'
```

Answer 1 (A) is the one that correctly will enable full text indexing for the database, setup a catalog, choose a table and create the index, and start it.

Question 30 - Administration

Every Monday you come and check your Maintenance Plans in your e-mail and the plan for msdb has failed. The maintenance plans include log backups for all databases. You know they reboot the server on Saturday. What could be the problem? *contributed by Chris Ammann.*

Choose one of the answers below:

1. Rebooting the server has set the Options tab for recovery to simple.
2. The reboot happened at the same time as the backup.
3. Your Maintenance Plan never worked. Go fix it!
4. The msdb database can't be backed up.

Answer:

1. Rebooting the server has set the Options tab for recovery to simple. The answer is #1. Rebooting the server has set the Options tab for recovery to simple. You have to go into properties and set the recovery to Full for the plan to work. You would not receive an error if SQLAgent did not start, so you can assume SQLAgent started with the reboot. Reference: INF: SQL Server Agent Automatically Sets "Trunc. Log on Chkpt" for MSDB, formerly Q257856.

Question 31 - Administration

You suspect that the indexes on your database have become somewhat fragmented and you want to defragment them. You are in the middle of a busy production cycle and want to make sure that the database stays as available as possible. What command would you use?
contributed by Kieth Rosman

Choose one of the answers below:

1. DBCC DBREINDEX
2. sp_configure
3. DBCC INDEXDEFRAG
4. sp_dbOptions ('tablename', fillfactor)

Answer:

3. DBCC INDEXDEFRAG
DBCC INDEXDEFRAG defragments both clusters and non-clustered indexes at the leaf level on tables and views while your database is online. If your indexes are not significantly fragmented it is a less burdomsome option than DBCC DBREINDEX and much less onerous than dropping and recreating the indexes.

Question 32 - Administration

What will be the output of the Following Statements if the same is pasted in the Query Analyzer ? (All 7 lines, including comments)

```
/*
select getdate()
go
select getdate()-1
go
*/
select getdate()+2
```

Choose one of the answers below:

1. Current date + 2
2. Current Date - 1
3. Error
4. Date Serial No.
5. Current date + 2 and current date -1
6. Current Date - 1 and an error

Answer:

6. Current Date - 1 and an error
as the Go ends the context of the Comment block it will return the error

```
Server: Msg 113, Level 15, State 1, Line 3
Missing end comment mark '*/'.

(1 row(s) affected)

Server: Msg 170, Level 15, State 1, Line 1
Line 1: Incorrect syntax near '*'.
```

but will execute the second line and retun the date -1.

Question 33 - Data Warehousing\Business Intelligence

How would you go about installing multiple instances of Analysis Services for SQL Server 2000 Standard Edition on a single server?

Choose one of the answers below:

1. You must upgrade to Analysis Services for SQL Server 2000 Enterprise Edition
2. You must specify a new port for each instances
3. Just install a new instance and name the instance
4. You cannot install multiple instances of Analysis Services

Answer:

4. You cannot install multiple instances of Analysis Services
You cannot install multiple instances of Analysis Services for SQL Server 2000. Because of this, you cannot place Analysis Services in an Active/Active cluster with another Analysis Services.
Ref: Analysis Services Setup -
http://msdn.microsoft.com/library/default.asp?url=/library/en-us/olapdmad/aginstalling_5trn.asp.

Question 34 - Data Warehousing\Business Intelligence

What firewall port(s) need to be opened for Analysis Services to communicate with both Analysis Services Clients and OLAP Services 7.0 Clients?

Question submitted by: Larry Briscoe
Choose one of the answers below:

1. TCP port 1433
2. TCP ports 2393 and 2394
3. TCP port 2725
4. TCP ports 2393, 2394 and 2725
5. TCP & UDP ports 2393 and 2394
6. TCP port 1433 and UDP port 1433

Answer:

4. TCP ports 2393, 2394 and 2725
Analysis Services uses TCP port 2725. For backward compatibility, Analysis Services also uses TCP ports 2393 and 2394 for connecting to an OLAP Services 7.0 Client.

Ref: INF: TCP Ports Used by OLAP Services when Connecting Through a Firewall - < a href="http://support.microsoft.com/default.aspx?scid=kb;en-us;301901">http://support.microsoft.com/default.aspx?scid=kb;en-us;301901 Note: Analysis Services also supports connections using HTTP using Microsoft IIS. TCP Ports Used by OLAP Services when Connecting Through a Firewall http://support.microsoft.com/default.aspx?scid=kb;EN-US;q301901

Question 35 - Data Warehousing\Business Intelligence

Which of the following storage models is a hybrid of a multidimensional and relational storage systems?

Choose one of the answers below:

1. ROLAP
2. MOLAP
3. HOLAP
4. YOLAP

Answer:

3. HOLAP
HOLAP is the hybrid model. A HOLAP storage design stores some of the cube data in a mutlidimensional model, the Analysis Services storage type and some of the data in a relational model. Ref: Analysis Services Architecture - http://msdn.microsoft.com/library/default.asp?url=/library/en-us/olapdmpr/printro_2k11.asp.

Question 36 - Disaster Recovery

You are the DBA for a large company with an OLTP application that handles the orders for your retail department. One of the applications creates named transactions that include the time in the name, such as price_update_0829_1005, for a transaction at 10:05 on 8/29. One of the finance people tells you that he just mistakenly completed a price update that set everything to the same price that needs to be rolled back. What can you do?
Choose one of the answers below:

1. Restore the database using point in time to 10:05.
2. Restore the database using the marked transaction restore feature.
3. Issue a "Rollback transaction to mark 'price_update_0829_1005'.
4. There is nothing you can do.

Answer:

2. Restore the database using the marked transaction restore feature. SQL Server does not allow you to rollback a single transaction. Third party products that do this, make a new transaction that reverses the changes made in the original transaction. You need to restore the database from backup to the named transaction. Note that there are many cases where you might do this. Support every item in your inventory was just set to the same name. The quickest recovery method might be restoring the db.

Question 37 - Disaster Recovery

Your SQL Server has just crashed and it's nearing the end of quarter. You implement the disaster recovery plan and begin restoring your .bak files from tape onto this server. Since this is a new Windows server (yo anticipate recovering the other server tomorrow), what must you do once you restore the master database from tape?

Choose one of the answers below:

1. Run sp_dropserver, sp_addserver
2. Restore model
3. Run "sqlsrvr -m -g" to run the SQL Server temporarily from a different Windows server.
4. Run "sp_disasterrecovery" to allow this SQL Server to run on a different Windows server.

Answer:

1. Run sp_dropserver, sp_addserver
You will need to run sp_dropserver, sp_addserver. Since this will be a temporary server, you are recovering the original tomorrow, and it is a NEW Windows server, the name stored in the SQL Server configuration will not match the underlying Windows server name. sp_dropserver, sp_addserver allow you to change this in SQL Server.

Question 38 - DMO

The abbreviation DMO means what in SQL 2000?

Choose one of the answers below:

1. Data Management Objects
2. Distributed Management Objects
3. Data Maintenance Objects
4. Distributed Maintenance Objects
5. Data Manipulation Online

Answer:

2. Distributed Management Objects
The correct answer is B, Distributed Management Objects. SQL-DMO gives programmers access to most of the functionality available in Enterprise Manager. None of the other answers are valid.

Question 39 - DMO

Using SQL-DMO, which of the following will allow you to connect using a trusted connection? The following code has been set up prior to this.

```
Dim oServer as SQLServer

Set Oserver = New SQLServer
```

Choose one of the answers below:

1. Oserver.connect “servername”
2. Oserver.loginsecure = false: oserver.connect “servername”
3. Oserver.UseTrustedConnection=True: oserver.connect “servername”
4. Oserver.LoginSecure = True:Oserver.connect “servername”

Answer:

4. Oserver.LoginSecure = True:Oserver.connect "servername"
Answer D is correct. You must set the loginsecure property to true, then call the connect method and pass in the servername. Answer A would fail unless you provided a sql userid and password. Answer B would fail because you explicitly said not to use a trusted connection. Answer C is not valid syntax.

Question 40 - DMO

You write a small VB6 utility app that will use SQL-DMO to connect to each of your production servers. During the standard pre-deployment code review one of your peers notes that you are not closing your DMO server connection properly. Which of the following is the correct way to close a server connection?

Choose one of the answers below:

1. set cn=nothing
2. oserver.disconnect: set oserver=nothing
3. oserver.closeconnection: set oserver=nothing
4. set oserver=nothing

Answer:

2. oserver.disconnect: set oserver=nothing
Answer B is correct. You should always explicitly call the disconnect method before setting your object to nothing. Answer A is ADO syntax, you are using DMO. Answer C is wrong because there is no closeconnection method. Answer D is incorrect because you should always call the disconnect method first.

Question 41 - DMO

You review some utility code that uses DMO and see a line that references the SQLServer2 object. What can you deduce about which version of DMO is being used?

Choose one of the answers below:

1. It is connected to the second server in the alphabetical list of servers on your network.
2. It is a copy of the server object in case you need to roll back changes.
3. Objects with a "2" suffix are part of DMO distributed with SQL 7
4. Objects with a "2" suffix are part of DMO distributed with SQL 2000.

Answer:

4. Objects with a "2" suffix are part of DMO distributed with SQL 2000.
Answer D is correct. To preserve backward compatibility objects that required changes in SQL 2000 (because of new capabilities) DMO has the original objects plus the "2" objects, where the ones ending in "2" are SQL 2000 specific. You should use the original objects if running on both SQL 7 and SQL 2000 is desired. Answer A could be correct, but you would have to have the list of servers to know that. Answer B is incorrect, even if you had copied the object it would be a pointer to the original object, not a true copy. Answer C is incorrect, "2" suffixes were added in SQL 2000.

Question 42 - DMO

You review a chunk of utility code and run across a DMO method call named ListAvailableSQLServers. Which of the following will happen when the code executes?

Choose one of the answers below:

1. It will return a list of all available servers on the network.
2. It will return a list of all SQL servers that advertise they are active.
3. It will return a list of all servers that support ANSI SQL on the network.
4. No such method call exists.

Answer:

2. It will return a list of all SQL servers that advertise they are active. Answer B is correct. As long as you have not checked the option to hide a server, the method call should identify the server. Answer A is incorrect because the method only targets SQL Servers. Answer C is incorrect because no other server types are supported whether they support ANSI SQL or not. Answer D is not a valid option.

Question 43 - DMO

Which of the following are capabilities of the SQLServer object in SQL-DMO?

Choose one of the answers below:

1. Connect to a server and start the service.
2. Connect to a server and stop the service.
3. Determine if the server has the DTC set to autostart.
4. Execute a SQL query.
5. Return a list of startup stored procedures.
6. All of the above.

Answer:

6. All of the above.

Answer H is correct. Using DMO you can stop, start, and pause the service. You can check the autostart status of the DTC (via the registry object that is part of the server object), execute a query, return the list of start up stored procedures, and check to see if you are a member of the syadmin role (or any other fixed role). Answer G is incorrect because you can execute a query using the ExecuteImmediate method.

Ref: SQLServer object - http://msdn.microsoft.com/library/default.asp?url=/library/en-us/sqldmo/dmoref_ob_s_7igk.asp.

Question 44 - DMO

What does the following code do?

```
Set oConfigValue =
oSQLServer.Configuration.ConfigValues("remote query timeout
(s)")
```

Choose one of the answers below:

1. Raises a dialog with the text "remote query timeout" and then displays the value of this parameter from the running configuration of the SQL Server whose handle is held by oSQLServer.
2. sets oConfigValue to a referenceto the value of this parameter from the running configuration of the SQL Server whose handle is held by oSQLServer. The parmaeter is the "Remote query timeout" value from sp_configure.
3. Sets the value of the SQL Server parameter, remote query timeout, to the value that is stored in oConfigValue.
4. It does nothing. This is syntactically incorrect.

Answer:

2. sets oConfigValue to a referenceto the value of this parameter from the running configuration of the SQL Server whose handle is held by oSQLServer. The parmaeter is the "Remote query timeout" value from sp_configure.
This snippet of SQL-DMO code retreives the configuration value for "remote query timeout(s)" that is set on the server whose handle is held by oSQLServer and stores it in the oConfigValue variable.

Question 45 - DTS

You are creating a DTS package in SQL Server 2000 and are ready to make it dynamic. In order to do this, you've created an Execute SQL task to accept a global variable as shown here:

SELECT * FROM AUTHORS WHERE AUTHORNM = ?
You then set the ? to be equal to a parameter called gvAuthorNm. How would you pass a global variable from the DTSRUN command into the package so it can be scheduled? For the purpose of this example, we'll use Brian as the variable we'd like to pass in.
Choose one of the answers below:

1. Use the following switch: /gvAuthorNm:"8"="Brian"
2. Use the following switch: /gvAuthorNm="Brian"
3. Use the following switch: /gvAuthorNm:"string"="Brian"
4. Use the following switch: /A "gvAuthorNm":"string"="Brian"
5. Use the following switch: /A "gvAuthorNm"="Brian"
6. Use the following switch: /A "gvAuthorNm":"8"="Brian"

Answer:

6. Use the following switch: /A "gvAuthorNm":"8"="Brian"
The benefit of the scenario above is the programmer can have one package that can be fired off many times and mean different things based on what parameter is passed in. You would use the /A switch to pass parameters into a DTS package. For more information, see http://www.sqlservercentral.com/faq/viewfaqanswer.asp?categoryid=2&faqid=17. Another hint is to go to DTSRUNUI and generate the command there in the Advanced area.
Ref: DTSRun Help - http://www.sqldts.com/?301.

Question 46 - DTS

You are a DTS programmer who wishes to output the status of the package's execution to a text file. You want to record whether or not a step executes to a text file. In SQL Server 2000, what is the easiest way to do this?

Choose one of the answers below:

1. In the package, go to Package Properties and click Log package execution to SQL Server under the Logging tab
2. In the package, go to Package Properties and click Log package execution to text file under the Logging tab
3. In the package, go to Package Properties and type a file destination in the Error file text box under the Logging tab
4. Right-click on the package and select Package Logs, specify a flat file location and click Save.

Answer:

3. In the package, go to Package Properties and type a file destination in the Error file text box under the Logging tab
Specify the name of the file where package and step status and error information will be written. This file will contain a list of the steps not executed, in addition to the steps that were executed and their result. The file can be on a local drive or on a mapped drive. If the file does not exist at package run time, the file will be created. The file does not have a default extension assigned to it; you must put the extension on the file name. The most common extension is .txt.
Ref: Logging Data Transformation Services Package Execution to a Text File - http://sqljunkies.com/How%20To/07DB1FCB-2F26-4A99-BD5F-15FA6F9F9B4A.scuk

Question 47 - DTS

I built a DTS transformation that exports data each day to an Excel spreadsheet. However the data is appended each day to the spreadsheet instead of replacing the existing data. What is wrong?

Choose one of the answers below:

1. Your DTS subsystem is corrupt and needs to be reinstalled.
2. You should uncheck the box on the Data Transform Options tab that says "Append Data"
3. You need to perform the equivalent of a truncate table on the spreadsheet.
4. This is a bug in DTS and a fix is supplied in SQL Server SP3.

Answer:

3. You need to perform the equivalent of a truncate table on the spreadsheet.
You need to remove the existing data, using the Excel automation model, copying a blank spreadsheet onto the target spreadsheet, or executing a drop table, create table on your spreadsheet.

Ref: HOW TO: Transfer Data to Excel by Using SQL Server Data Transformation Services - http://support.microsoft.com/default.aspx?scid=kb;EN-US;319951

Question 48 - DTS

Examine the following two SQL statements. Why would SQL statement A return a value in Query Analyzer, but when run from within Dynamic Properties of a SQL Server 2000 DTS package it returns neither an error nor any values?

SQL Statement A:

```
Select '\\nat1-iac5-sql\k$\production\output\client\'
+ convert(varchar(6), convert(varchar(6), getdate(),
112) - 1) + '\client_output_' + convert(varchar(12),
getdate(), 112)
  + '.mdb'
```

Although SQL Statement B below returns values in both, Query Analyzer and from within Dynamic Properties of DTS package.

SQL Statement B:

```
select '\\nat1-iac5-sql\k$\production\output\client\'
+ convert(varchar(6), convert(varchar(6), getdate(),
112) - 1) + '\client_output_' + convert(varchar(12),
getdate(), 112)
   + '.zip \\nat1-iac5-
sql\k$\production\output\client\'
   + convert(varchar(6), convert(varchar(6),
getdate(),
112) - 1)+ '\client_output_' + convert(varchar(12),
getdate(), 112) + '.mdb'
```

Choose one of the answers below:

1. This issue is a bug in DTS.
2. This issue is a bug in Query Analyzer.
3. It is a trick question. Both statements work in Query Analyzer and DTS.
4. You cannot put this statement in a Dynamic Properties task. It is too long.

Answer:

1. This issue is a bug in DTS.
This is due to a BUG in DTS, confirmed by Microsoft. A discussion is available at
http://www.dbforums.com/showthread.php?threadid=656046&goto=nextoldest

For SQL Statement A to return any values from within Dynamic Properties of a DTS package, it has to be modified as following:

```
SQL Statement A  (Modified)

Select
cast('\\nat1-iac5-sql\k$\production\output\client\' as
varchar(1000)) + convert(varchar(6),
convert(varchar(6), getdate(), 112) - 1) +
'\client_output_' + convert(varchar(12), getdate(),
112) + '.mdb'
```

Question 49 - Enterprise Administration

You need to move a virtual instance of SQL server from Node 1 to Node2 within a cluster, but you need to schedule a time to run the task during the non-production time instead of using the Microsoft Management Console. What command would you issue?

Windows cluster name : SQLCluster
Group to move: SQLVS1
Node to move it to: Node2
Choose one of the answers below:

1. Issue a NET STOP command on the node that you'd like to move
2. Issue the command: Cluster SQLCluster group "SQLVS1" /MOVETO:Node2
3. Issue the command: Cluster SQLVS1 group SQLCluster /MOVETO:Node2
4. Issue the command: clusvr SQLCluster group "SQLVS1" /MOVETO:Node2
5. Issue the command: clusvr SQLVS1 group SQLCluster /MOVETO:Node2

Answer:

2. Issue the command: Cluster SQLCluster group "SQLVS1" /MOVETO:Node2

To fail the server over using a schedule, you'd need to know the line command and issue the cluster statement with the proper parameters. The first parameter in the cluster command specifies the windows cluster virtual name, then the group command and name. Lastly, you must specify the moveto command and what node to move it to.

Question 50 - Enterprise Administration

You are a DBA of a SQL Server environment that's clustered. Periodically, your Full Text resource will fail, causing your entire SQL Server cluster group to fail over to the other node and causing an outage for a few minutes. The Full Text resource is not critical to you and you want to allow it to fail without causing a complete SQL Server failure. How could you do this?

Choose one of the answers below:

1. Adjust the dependencies to where SQL Server no longer relates to Full Text
2. Uncheck "Affect the Group" option in the Full Text resource properties
3. Modify a registry setting under the Full Text service tree.
4. Move Full Text out of the cluster group with SQL Server

Answer:

2. Uncheck "Affect the Group" option in the Full Text resource properties

For each resource in a cluster group, the default behavior is to fail the entire group over as soon as it senses a problem with a single resource. This may or may not be the bahavior you'd like to see exhibited. Some services like Full Text and sql Server Agent you would not want to fail over the entire group. To fix this, right-click on the resource and go to Properties. Then unselect Affect The Group in the third tab.

Ref: Failver Cluster Troubleshooting -
http://msdn.microsoft.com/library/default.asp?url=/library/en-us/adminsql/ad_clustering_87vr.asp.

Question 51 - Enterprise Administration

You need to discover which instances of SQL Server are running our your large network. You can connect to a few test servers (default instances) in a lab using TCP/IP sockets. When you try to browse the named instances on a production server from a different subnet, you cannot find any instances running. You are sure that the named instance SQLDB01\DW_Finance is running. What could be the problem?

Choose one of the answers below:

1. UDP Port 1434 is not open on your router.
2. TCP Port 1434 is not open on your router
3. You do not have the proper authority to connect to that instance of SQL Server.
4. Your AD group policy prohibits you from connecting to that SQL Server.

Answer:

1. UDP Port 1434 is not open on your router.
To find out which named instances are running, your workstation will connect to UDP Port 1434 to get a list of instances and the ports on which they are listening. Since the named instances dynamically choose a port when they start up, you need 1434 to determine the port remotely.

Ref: Open UDP Port 1434 to Browse Named Instances
http://www.microsoft.com/sql/techinfo/tips/administration/port1434.asp.

Question 52 - Enterprise Administration

From time to time, we add new SAN drives onto a clustered SQL Server. You want to distribute your database across additional disk drives on your cluster. You've detached the database and move the physical files to the new drives. When you go back to your Enterprise Manager to reattach the db's, you can't see the new drives. What's you most likely problem?

Choose one of the answers below:

1. The disks were configured as dynamic drives and only basic drives are allowed in clusters.
2. The disks were configured as basic drives and only dynamic drives are allowed in clusters.
3. The drive resources are not in the dependency list for the SQL Server resource for the cluster.
4. You need to restart SQL Server to see the drives.

Answer:

3. The drive resources are not in the dependency list for the SQL Server resource for the cluster.
From time to time, we add new SAN drives onto a clustered SQL Server. When we spread the databases out, or add filegroups or databases, nobody ever remembers to add the disk resources to the dependency list for the SQL Server resource

Question 53 - Replication

Transactional replication offers the option to replicate views and stored procedures along with tables. Using SQL 2000, what will happen if you alter a stored procedure that has been included in a transactional publication?

Choose one of the answers below:

1. The change will be replicated to all subscribers
2. The change will be replicated to SQL 2000 subscribers
3. You cannot alter a stored procedure that is replicated
4. You can alter the stored procedure but you have to manually apply the change to all subscribers.

Answer:

4. You can alter the stored procedure but you have to manually apply the change to all subscribers.

Answer D is correct. Stored procedures can be included as part of a publication and will be applied to the subscriber when a snapshot is done but changes are not replicated after that. There is no restriction on altering stored procedures that are part of a publication.

Question 54 - Replication

Using SQL 2000, a single instance can act in which of the following replication roles?

Choose one of the answers below:

1. Publisher
2. Distributor
3. Subscriber
4. Printer
5. A, B, and C
6. A and B only

Answer:

5. A, B, and C
Answers A, B, and C are correct. It is possible (and common) for a server to act as a Publisher and Distributor at the same time. It is also possible to have it be a Subscriber to publications published on the same instance. Answer D is incorrect because there is not a role named Printer. Answer E is correct.

Question 55 - Replication

The log reader agent runs until stopped when you set up a transactional publication in SQL 2000. What will happen if you stop SQL Agent to investigate an unrelated problem and forget to restart it?

Choose one of the answers below:

1. You'll be fired for being a bonehead.
2. The job will not run of course, which means that no transactions will be sent to the subscribers.
3. The log reader has nothing to do with SQL Agent, you can tell because it shows up in a different part of Enterprise Manager.
4. The log reader will restart itself automatically.

Answer:

2. The job will not run of course, which means that no transactions will be sent to the subscribers.
Answer B is correct. Answer A is likely, but it depends on how long it takes you to remember to restart SQL Agent. Answer C is wrong because while you do administer the log reader under the replication node of EM, it is really just a link to a standard job that requires the agent to be running (or you to be smarter than the average bear). Answer D is incorrect, the log reader has no ability to detect that it is not running.

Question 56 - Replication

You create a transactional publication in SQL 2000 that contains one table called Customers and set up a single subscriber. The primary key on that table is also an identity column. What will happen if you attempt to insert a row into the subscriber copy of Customers using Query Analyzer and do not provide a value for the primary key?

Choose one of the answers below:

1. The insert will succeed because SQL will generate an identity value automatically.
2. The insert will succeed because an instead of trigger on the subscriber forces the insert to be done on the publisher and then replicated back to the subscriber.
3. The insert will fail because the identity property is not set on the subscriber table.
4. No direct inserts are allowed, all changes have be done at the publisher.

Answer:

3. The insert will fail because the identity property is not set on the subscriber table.

Answer C is correct. Answer A is correct because the identity setting is not copied to the subscriber so unless you provide a value for the column the insert will fail. Answer B is incorrect (though you could make it work as long as you could support a distributed transaction, it is not the default behavior). Answer D is incorrect; you can make changes at any time directly to the subscriber.

Question 57 - Replication

Which of the following statements are true about subscribers to a standard transactional publication in SQL 2000?

Choose one of the answers below:

1. Changes made to the subscriber will be replicated back to the publisher.
2. Changes cannot be made to a table that is part of a transactional publication.
3. Changes can be made with no ill effect.
4. Changes can be made but may cause issues.
5. Subscribers require an additional license before they can be updated.

Answer:

4. Changes can be made but may cause issues.
Answer D is correct. Changing data on the subscriber may result in errors later when changes are applied, it will also cause validation to fail unless the same changes are applied to the publisher. Answer A is not correct because a standard publication does not have the immediately updating subscriber option set. Answer B is just plain wrong. Answer C is incorrect because at a minimum changing data on the subscriber will cause validation to fail (with the caveat noted earlier). Answer E is incorrect; no additional licenses are required.

Question 58 - Replication

You have a SQL 2000 transactional publication that has a failing distribution agent, the error message indicates that it is because it attempted to insert a duplicate primary key on the subscriber. Which of the following will correct the problem?

Choose one of the answers below:

1. Add the –skiperrors flag to the distribution agent, and then restart the agent.
2. Reinitialize the publication, and then start the snapshot agent.
3. Delete the duplicate row from the subscriber, and then restart the agent.
4. Modify the insert stored proc on the subscriber to not fail if the row already exists.
5. All of the above.

Answer:

5. All of the above.

Answer E is correct. Setting skiperrors is quick, but should normally be turned back off once the problem has been fixed or you may miss other more important errors. Reinitializing and doing a new snapshot will always work, but will take longer than any of the other options unless it is a very small table. Deleting the row from the subscriber is quick and effective unless there are hundreds of duplicates – you have to identify each one as it happens, delete it, try the agent again. Modifying the stored procedure on the subscriber is also fast but has the same downside as using skiperrors, you may want to know when the problem has occurred. The other problem with this solution is that if you do a new snapshot your change will be lost.

Question 59 - Replication

You build a transactional publication in SQL 2000 and select the option to have it run once per hour. When you check the status of the jobs in SQL Agent you see that the log reader job never ends – why?

Choose one of the answers below:

1. There are a lot of transactions to process; the agent just has not caught up yet.
2. The job is hung, restart SQL Agent.
3. You don't have sufficient permissions to set up the publication correctly.
4. Even though you set a schedule it only affects the distribution agent.

Answer:

4. Even though you set a schedule it only affects the distribution agent. Answer D is correct. By default the log reader runs continuously regardless of the schedule setting selected. Answer A is incorrect because the job will not stop until it receives a stop request. Answer B is incorrect, even if you restarted SQL Agent or rebooted the server the logreader would exhibit the same behavior when it started again. Answer C is incorrect, the issue has nothing to do with permissions.

Question 60 - Reporting Services

You have recently installed SQL Server 2000 Reporting Services and you are now finalizing your installation. During setup, you did not specify the correct mail server to send reports out of and you need to change it. How would you go about configuring the mail server setup for Reporting Services?

Choose one of the answers below:

1. Open the Administration console in Internet Explorer and select Administration Options and Mail Delivery
2. Modify the global.asa in the \Reporting Services\ReportManager folder
3. Modify the RSReportServer.config in the \Reporting Services\ReportServer folder.
4. Modify the web.config in the \Reporting Services\ReportManager folder
5. You must reinstall Reporting Services

Answer:

3. Modify the RSReportServer.config in the \Reporting Services\ReportServer folder.
The answer is to modify the RSReportServer.config file located at:
C:\Program Files\Microsoft SQL Server\MSSQL\Reporting Services\ReportServer\

You change the SMTP setting in this file.

Ref: Configuring a Report Server for E-Mail Delivery - http://msdn.microsoft.com/library/default.asp?url=/library/en-us/rsadmin/htm/arp_configserver_v1_4bzl.asp.

Question 61 - Reporting Services

True or false? SQL Reporting Services has to be installed on a machine with SQL Server installed?

Choose one of the answers below:

1. True
2. False

Answer:

2. False

Answer: 'False'. You need a SQL Server 2000 license for the machine on which it is installed, and you need a SQL Server 2000 machine to host the ReportServer and ReportServerTempDB databases, but Reporting Services does not have to be on the same physical box as your SQL Server.

Ref: Deployment Guide (http://www.microsoft.com/technet/prodtechnol/sql/2000/deploy/rsdepgd.mspx).

Question 62 - Reporting Services

True or False? MSDE and SQL Server Personal Edition can be used as a source of data for reports.

Choose one of the answers below:

1. True
2. False

Answer:

1. True

Answer: 'True' The report server database is a SQL Server database that stores data used by a report server. MSDE and SQL Server Personal Edition cannot host the report server database, though it can be used as a source of data for the reports.

Ref: SQL Server™ 2000 Reporting Services Deployment Guide (http://www.microsoft.com/technet/prodtechnol/sql/2000/deploy/rsdepgd.mspx).

Question 63 - Reporting Services

In Reporting Services 2000, the connection information used during setup for the report server has changed and you want to modify the connection information. Which utility allows you to do this?

Choose one of the answers below:

1. RS utility
2. RSACTIVATE utility
3. RSCONFIG utility
4. RSKEYMGMT utility
5. RSCONNECT utility

Answer:

3. RSCONFIG utility

The connection information used to establish the connection is initially defined during setup. However, if you want to modify the connection information, or if you are moving components to different computers, you can run rsconfig to correct it. There is no such utility as RSCONNECT. Ref: rsconfig(http://msdn.microsoft.com/library/default.asp?url=/library/en-us/RSUIREF/htm/cpu_rsconfig_v1_5f1e.asp).

Question 64 - Reporting Services

You create a report that has a title, and 2 sub-reports. The 2 sub-reports utilise a shared data source. Where is that data source stored?

Choose one of the answers below:

1. Within the main Report.
2. Within the sub-reports themselves.
3. A separate file.

Answer:

3. A separate file.
Answer: A separate file. A data source can be contained solely within a single report, or it can be shared by several reports. The definition for a report-specific data source is stored within the report itself, while the definition for a shared data source is stored in a separate file on the report server. A report can contain one data source (report-specific or shared) or many.

Ref: Shared Data Sources and Report-Specific Data Sources - http://msdn.microsoft.com/library/default.asp?url=/library/en-us/rswork/htm/rms_datasources_v1_33oi.asp.

Question 65 - Security

What is the minimum permissions you would need to create a new database?

Choose one of the answers below:

1. db_dbowner
2. Disk Administrators
3. Database Creators
4. System Administrators
5. Database Administrators
6. Setup Administrators
7. db_ddladmin

Answer:

3. Database Creators
The Database Creators server role allows you to be able to create and alter databases. You can also do this with the System Administrator role, but that will give the login unlimitted rights.

Ref: Create Database - http://msdn.microsoft.com/library/default.asp?url=/library/en-us/tsqlref/ts_create_1up1.asp

Question 66 - SQL Server Development

You recently took over a SQL server 2000 server that supported a legacy set of databases. when you ran the following new query against the database inside a stored procedure:

SELECT TOP 10 * FROM Orders
you receive the following error:
Server: Msg 170, Level 15, State 1, Line 1
Line 1: Incorrect syntax near '10'.
What would be one of the first areas to troubleshoot?
Choose one of the answers below:

1. The query has an invalid query hint in it
2. Check the database compatibility level
3. Check the stored procedure compatibility level
4. Check the table compatibility level
5. Check your SQL Server Service Pack to ensure you're on SP2 or greater
6. None of the above

Answer:

2. Check the database compatibility level
One problem that may arise when selecting based on the TOP clause is compatibility levels. If your compatibility level for the database is set to anything below 70 (SQL Server 7.0), the TOP clause does not work. For example, if you run the following query:
SELECT TOP 10 * FROM Orders
you may receive the following error:
Server: Msg 170, Level 15, State 1, Line 1
Line 1: Incorrect syntax near '10'.
If you receive this, immediately run the following query to check the compatibility level of the database:
SP_DBCMPTLEVEL 'Northwind'
You see the following result if the level is not set appropriately:
The current compatibility level is 65. To set the compatibility level back to SQL Server 2000 level, you can use the same stored procedure with the added parameter '80', which represents the version
SP_DBCMPTLEVEL 'Northwind', '80'

Question 67 - SQL Server Development

You have the following objects in one SQL Server 2000 database:

```
CREATE TABLE DebugMe (RecordNumber int NOT NULL
IDENTITY (1,1), MyComments varchar(50))
GO

CREATE UNIQUE INDEX IX_MyComments ON DebugMe
(MyComments) WITH FILLFACTOR = 100 ON [PRIMARY]
GO

CREATE TRIGGER IAlwaysFire ON DebugMe
FOR INSERT, UPDATE, DELETE
AS

UPDATE DebugMe SET MyComments = MyComments + '
IAlwaysFire was here.'
GO

CREATE PROCEDURE RunMe (@MyComments varchar(20) =
'None entered by user.')
AS


INSERT INTO DebugMe (MyComments)
VALUES (@MyComments)
GO
```

You execute in Query Analyzer this code twice: EXEC RunMe. The first execution runs fine. The second time you run it you get the following error:

```
Server: Msg 8152, Level 16, State 9, Procedure
IAlwaysFire, Line 6
String or binary data would be truncated.
The statement has been terminated.
```

Why did you get this error

Contributed by Robert Marda

Choose one of the answers below:

1. SQL Server did not have enough space to add the new row to the index.

2. The default value in the stored procedure exceeds the number of characters allowed by the column MyComments.

3. The trigger tried to update the column MyComments with more than 50 characters.

4. The insert statement in the stored procedure tried to insert more then 50 characters into the column MyComments.

Answer:

3. The trigger tried to update the column MyComments with more than 50 characters.

Here is what happened. The first execution of the SP RunMe added one row to the table DebugMe. The number of characters in MyComments is 42. 20 are from the default value in the SP. The other 22 were added by the trigger. The second time you run the SP, the trigger attempts to add another 22 characters to the column MyComments in the one existing row in table DebugMe. The total would be 64 which exceeds the max of 50 and so the trigger causes the error and rollsback the update it was trying to do and the second insert the SP tried to do.

Question 68 - SQL Server Development

A developer in your company has created a number of tables and you now need to create stored procedures against the tables. One such table that was created by the developer was called Employees. When you attempt to select against the table though Query Analyzer returns the error:

Server: Msg 208, Level 16, State 1, Line 1
Invalid object name 'Employees'.
What is the most likely cause of the error (note: the developer can see the table fine)?
Choose one of the answers below:

1. Your user must be in the db_datareader group to select against the table
2. The developer has to create the stored procedures since he created the tables
3. You must specify the table owner in your select statement
4. Your user doesn't have SELECT rights to view the table
5. The collation of your account doesn't match the original developer's

Answer:

3. You must specify the table owner in your select statement
The most likely cause of the error involves table ownership. Since the developer created the table, you can assume that he created it when signed in with his login. This will create the table like this DeveloperLogin.Employees instead of just Employees. You can either call the fully qualified table name or just change the table ownership to dbo.

Question 69 - SQL Server Development

You are a UNIX developer who is developing an application to use SQL Server 2000. What is the easiest, most cost-effective way to communicate to your SQL Server from UNIX.

Choose one of the answers below:

1. Windows Services for UNIX
2. Host Integration Server
3. In the Control Panel | Data Sources
4. The SQL Server 2000 Driver for JDBC
5. All the above

Answer:

4. The SQL Server 2000 Driver for JDBC
The Microsoft SQL Server 2000 Driver for JDBC is a Type 4 JDBC driver that provides scalable connectivity for the Java environment in Unix flavors or Windows. This driver provides JDBC access to SQL Server 2000, both 32 bit and 64 bit editions, through any Java-enabled applet, application, or application server. The drive is freely downloadable from http://www.microsoft.com/sql for more details.

Question 70 - SQL Server Development

You are a SQL Server developer who is developing an XPath query. You want the SQL Server to use more caching though for your XDR schema. How would you go about increasing this type of caching?

Choose one of the answers below:

1. Change an option using sp_configure
2. Change the server properties under the General tab
3. Use the SET CACHESIZE command
4. Modify or add the HKEY_LOCAL_MACHINE\SOFTWARE\Microsoft\MSSQLServer\Client\SQLXMLX\SchemaCacheSize data key

Answer:

4. Modify or add the HKEY_LOCAL_MACHINE\SOFTWARE\Microsoft\MSSQLServer\Client\SQLXMLX\SchemaCacheSize data key

Schema caching significantly improves the performance of an XPath query. When an XPath query is executed against an annotated XDR schema, the schema is stored in memory, and the necessary data structures are built in memory. If schema caching is set, the schema remains in memory, thereby improving performance for subsequent XPath queries.

You can set the schema cache size by adding the following key in the registry:

HKEY_LOCAL_MACHINE\SOFTWARE\Microsoft\MSSQLServer\Client\SQLXMLX\SchemaCacheSize.

The schema size is set based on the available memory and the number of schemas you are using. The default SchemaCacheSize size is 31. If you set SchemaCacheSize higher, more memory is used. Therefore, you can increase the cache size if schema access seems slow, or decrease the cache size if memory is low.

For performance reasons, it is recommended that you set SchemaCacheSize higher than the number of mapping schemas you usually use. As the number of schemas increase, if SchemaCacheSize is less than the number of schemas you have, the performance degrades.

Ref: Schema Caching - http://msdn.microsoft.com/library/default.asp?url=/library/en-us/sqlxml3/htm/otherimprovements_5hbb.asp

Question 71 - SQL Server Development

You are a developer who is developing who uses English Query frequently in your applicaton to make a better user experience. You have now been tasked with translating the application to Spanish and need English Query to also accept Spanish questions. How would you accomplish this in SQL Server English Query?

Choose one of the answers below:

1. Install the Spanish version of SQL Server 2000
2. Change the locale ID on the database server
3. Issue a SET LANGUAGE command in T-SQL
4. Modify a registry key
5. Change the SQL Server collation
6. English Query only works in English and your goal cannot be met with this product

Answer:

6. English Query only works in English and your goal cannot be met with this product
As the product name implies, at this time, there isn't a multilingual version of English Query.

Question 72 - SQL Server Development

Your company sells gasoline to commercial construction companies at a steep discount. Recently your boss landed a contract with a small landscaping company and has come to you with a problem. Prior to this contract, all sales were in whole gallon amounts with any partials being rounded up to the next gallon. However with this new contact, partial gallon amounts can be sold. When someone was entering a sale for 5.5 gallons, they received an error in the application.

You check and determine that the table holding the sales stores the number of gallons in the totgallons field, which is a smallint and has a default of zero (0). You need to alter this to be a numeric(8,2). Which statement will do this?

Here is a partial DDL:

```
CREATE TABLE [SalesItem] (
    [TotGal] [smallint] NOT NULL CONSTRAINT
[DF_SalesItem_TotGal] DEFAULT (0),
) ON [PRIMARY]
GO
```

Choose one of the answers below:

1.

```
ALTER TABLE [salesitem]
    ALTER COLUMN TotGal numeric(8,2)
GO
```

2.

```
ALTER TABLE [salesitem] DROP CONSTRAINT
DF_SalesItem_TotGal
GO
ALTER TABLE [salesitem]
    ALTER COLUMN TotGal numeric(8,2)
GO
```

3.

```
ALTER TABLE [salesitem] DROP CONSTRAINT
DF_SalesItem_TotGal
GO
ALTER TABLE [salesitem]
    ALTER COLUMN TotGal numeric(8,2)
GO
ALTER TABLE [salesitem] ADD CONSTRAINT
```

```
    DF_salesitem_TotGal DEFAULT 0 FOR TotGal
GO
```

4.

```
ALTER TABLE [salesitem]
    ALTER COLUMN TotGal numeric(8,2) WITH DEFAULT
```

Answer:

3.

```
ALTER TABLE [salesitem] DROP CONSTRAINT
DF_SalesItem_TotGal
GO
ALTER TABLE [salesitem]
    ALTER COLUMN TotGal numeric(8,2)
GO
ALTER TABLE [salesitem] ADD CONSTRAINT
    DF_salesitem_TotGal DEFAULT 0 FOR TotGal
GO
```

To alter a column that has a default constraint, you must first remove the constraint, and then add it back.

Question 73 - SQL Server Development

What is one of the reasons that the first procedure below might perform better than the second in an OLTP environment?

```
create procedure MyOrder
   @orderid int
as
select OrderID, CustomerID, OrderDate
 from dbo.Orders
 where OrderID = @OrderID
GO

create procedure MyOrder
   @orderid int
as
select OrderID, CustomerID, OrderDate
 from Orders
 where OrderID = @OrderID
GO
```

Choose one of the answers below:

1. They will always perform the same.
2. It won't. The second one will perform better because it has less characters and will execute faster.
3. The second procedure may be recompiled because the owner is not specified.
4. It will always depend on the indexing on the Orders table.

Answer:

3. The second procedure may be recompiled because the owner is not specified.
If the owner of the table is not specified, the query optimizer must determine that user Steve is accessing dbo.Orders and not Steve.Orders. This can cause a recompilation of the stored procedure, reducing performance. Microsoft has written a tip on this:Coding an Owner to Avoid Recompilation.

Question 74 - SQL Server Development

Can you use an ORDER BY clause in this view definition?

```
create view NorthView
as
select accountID, Customer, Balance
 from Accounts
 where region = 'North'
go
```

Choose one of the answers below:

1. Yes
2. No

Answer:

1. Yes
If you include the TOP command, you can include an ORDER BY clause in a view definition, however the definition given would not be allowed.

Ref: CREATE VIEW - http://msdn.microsoft.com/library/default.asp?url=/library/en-us/tsqlref/ts_create2_30hj.asp

Question 75 - SQL Server Development

Can you please define covering indexes?
Submitted by Ronald Cartmale

Choose one of the answers below:

1. An index that is used on every query.
2. An index whose columns are all used in the WHERE clause. So a 2 column index would have both columns mentioned in the WHERE clause.
3. An index whose columns are used in the WHERE clause and also are the only columns returned in the SELECT clause.
4. An index that can be used on more than one query.

Answer:

3. An index whose columns are used in the WHERE clause and also are the only columns returned in the SELECT clause.
Covering an index means that you're covering certain queries. What it means is instead of running those queries you can define an index on those queries, and the index is going to cover what a query is going to return the data on. The best way to describe this is if you're doing a SELECT statement and you have a certain value on it, the covering index is going to cover that query; the index is going to return the data, and that index is going to cover the result, whatever the query is going to return the data on. The best place to see this is in a demo. But the best resource on covering indexes is the SQL Server Books Online. That resource will be much more descriptive.

Question 76 - SQL Server Development

In SQL Server 2000, the datetime datatype handles values down to milliseconds. However the precision is not what you might accept. For the millisecond digit, which of the following values is NOT valid for the datetime datatype?

Choose one of the answers below:

1. 6
2. 0
3. 3
4. 7

Answer:

1. 6

All datetime values are rounded to the nearest 300th of a second. So the only possible values are 0, 3, and 7. Therefore 6 is not a possible value as anything above .005 seconds is rounded to .007.

Ref:Datetime data - http://msdn.microsoft.com/library/default.asp?url=/library/en-us/tsqlref/ts_da-db_9xut.asp from BOL.

Question 77 - SQL Server Development

```
SET datefirst 7
Declare @Dw as Int,
   @Dt as Datetime
Set @Dt = '09/04/2004'
Set @Dw = DATEPART(dw, @Dt)
Select @Dw as [Day of Week]
```

What will this return? (assume the date format is mm/dd/yyyy)

Contributed by Necrossomus

Choose one of the answers below:

1. 3
2. 7
3. 1
4. 5

Answer:

2. 7
"7" will be returned. The Datepart function returns a numeric result for the part of the date. The dw argument returns the day of the week. By setting datefirst as 7, then Sunday is 1 and Saturday is 7. The 4th of September of 2004 was a Saturday. See Datepart - http://msdn.microsoft.com/library/default.asp?url=/library/en-us/tsqlref/ts_da-db_2mic.asp
and datefirst - http://msdn.microsoft.com/library/default.asp?url=/library/en-us/tsqlref/ts_set-set_4qic.asp.

Question 78 - T-SQL

This is the data in the myOrders table

```
Order_No                  Unique_ID
------------------------- -----------
RON                       1
BILL                      2
FRED                      3
```

This is the data in the myItems table

```
Order_No               Item_No     Unique_ID
---------------------- ----------- -----------
RON                    1           1
RON                    2           2
RON                    3           3
RON                    4           4
BILL                   1           5
BILL                   2           6
BILL                   3           7
BILL                   4           8
FRED                   1           9
FRED                   2           10
FRED                   3           11
FRED                   4           12
```

Study the following two SQL Statements, SQL Statement A:-

```
SQL Statement A:-
select myOrd.Order_No, myiT.Item_No, myOrd.Unique_ID
as 'UniqueID'
FROM myOrders myOrd
JOIN myItems myiT
ON myOrd.Order_No = myiT.Order_No
Order BY myiT.Unique_ID desc
```

SQL Statement B:-

```
select myOrd.Order_No, myiT.Item_No, myOrd.Unique_ID
as 'Unique_ID'
FROM myOrders myOrd
JOIN myItems myiT
ON myOrd.Order_No = myiT.Order_No
Order BY myiT.Unique_ID desc
```

QUESTION:- What will they SQL Statements return?

Choose one of the answers below:

1. identical recordsets?
2. SQL Statement A will return its recordset sorted by the Alias 'Unique_ID' descending , SQL Statement B:- will return it recordset sorted by myiT.Unique_ID descending
3. SQL Statement A will return its recordset sorted by myiT.Unique_ID descending , SQL Statement B:- will return it recordset sorted by the Alias 'Unique_ID' descending
4. SQL Statement B will generate a syntax error

Answer:

3. SQL Statement A will return its recordset sorted by myiT.Unique_ID descending , SQL Statement B:- will return it recordset sorted by the Alias 'Unique_ID' descending
This was submitted by Ronald C. crafted two statements that are slightly different, but it is easy to misread. The alias is different for the two tables, resulting in different ordering.

Question 79 - T-SQL

You have created the following view?

```
create view MyOrders
as
select c.customername, c.customerid
   , o.orderdate, o.ordercost, o.status
 from customers c
    inner join orders o
               on c.customerid = o.customerid
```

You want to issue this statement:

```
update MyOrders
 set customername = 'NewGuy'
  , orderdate = getdate()
   where customerid = 'New'
```

Will this work?

Choose one of the answers below:

1. You cannot do this as the view contains multiple tables.
2. You cannot do this as the update references two tables.
3. This will work fine.

Answer:

2. You cannot do this as the update references two tables.
You can only update a single table at a time in this view. With other more complicated views, such as updateable partitioned views, it would be possible to update more than one table.

The answer specifying the view containing more than one table is not correct because views can legally contain more than one table, and you can update through them. The update would not fail because the view had more than one table, but rather because the update referenced two base tables.

Question 80 - T-SQL

You have created the following view?

```
create view MyOrders
as
select c.customername, c.customerid
    , o.orderdate, o.ordercost, o.status
 from customers c
    inner join orders o
               on c.customerid = o.customerid
```

You want to update the Orders table through this view. Can you do this?

Choose one of the answers below:

1. You cannot do this as the view contains multiple tables.
2. You can update the orders table as long as the update only updates the orderdate, ordercost, or status columns.
3. You can update any column in the orders table as long as you only update the orders table.

Answer:

2. You can update the orders table as long as the update only updates the orderdate, ordercost, or status columns.
You can update a view that contains multiple tables as long as you only update a single table at a time. If you attempt to update other columns from the orders table through the view, you will receive the "invalid column name" error.

Question 81 - T-SQL

When we add a new column with default value 'N' to the existing table which already has rows. Will the existing rows for the new column automatically change to 'N'? NULLs are allowed on the new column.

Choose one of the answers below:

1. Yes
2. No

Answer:

2. No
SQL Server will not automatically update exisiting records with the default value of an added new column. We need to manually change it using an update statement if we want all the rows set to 'N'.

Question 82 - T-SQL

What would the following SQL statement do on SQL Server 2000?

```
CREATE DATABASE GO
```

Choose one of the answers below:

1. fail to compile
2. attempt to create an unnamed database and fail.
3. Create a database called go.

Answer:

3. Create a database called go.
SQL Server will create a database called "go". Like in many functions, keywords are sometimes ignored if they "fit" within the framework of the command. The create database command expects a parameter for the database name, all other parameters being optional. Since "go" fits that spot, it's used before being parsed as a batch separation marker.

Question 83 - T-SQL

On SQL 2000 approximately what is the default maximum size limit for replicating a single write to a text/image field?

Choose one of the answers below:

1. Unlimited
2. 2Gb, the maximum permitted size of a text/image field.
3. 1MB
4. 64Kb
5. 8Kb

Answer:

4. 64Kb
Answer is 64kb or 65536 bytes.

This can be overridden using

```
exec sp_configure 'max text repl size' , '<>'
RECONFIGURE WITH OVERRIDE
```

Question 84 - T-SQL

Which of the following queries will allow you to check if you have already created a temporary table called #mytable

Choose one of the answers below:

1. IF EXISTS(SELECT 1 FROM tempdb.dbo.sysobjects WHERE name = '#mytable') PRINT 'Already created'
2. IF EXISTS(SELECT 1 FROM #mytable) PRINT 'Already created'
3. IF OBJECT_ID('tempdb..#mytable') IS NOT NULL PRINT 'Already created'
4. The task can not be achieved?

Answer:

3. IF OBJECT_ID('tempdb..#mytable') IS NOT NULL PRINT 'Already created'
Answer A will not work as the temporary table name in tempdb..sysobjects has a unique identifier appended to it so that multiple users can create temporary tables

Answer B will create an error if the table does not exist.

Answer C works and will only detect your copy of #mytable.

Answer D is In correct.

Question 85 - T-SQL

Which of the following queries will return the message @myvariable is null?

declare @myvariable int

Choose one of the answers below:

1. IF @myvariable = NULL Print '@myvariable is null'
2. IF @myvariable is null Print '@myvariable is null'
3. SELECT isnull(@myvariable,'@myvariable is null')

Answer:

2. IF @myvariable is null Print '@myvariable is null'
The local variable @myvariable has been declared but not initialised. Had it been initialised to NULL then both answer a) and b) would work wheras answer c) will always result in a syntax error.

The reason is the difference between how = NULL and is null works.

SQL variables consist of two parts, the actual memory in which the value is physically held and a pointer to the value's memory location.

When a parameter is declared, a pointer of the data type is allocated by SQL but remains undefined. The is null function checks both the pointer and the data values, and if either are null then the statement returns true and in answer c will return the message.

The = NULL simply checks that the value of the parameter is actually assigned to NULL.and so answer a) will not return the message.

Question 86 - T-SQL

You are using SQL Server 2000, and wish to query a linked server. To do this you open Enterprise Manager and use it to create the following stored procedure:

```
CREATE PROCEDURE dbo.spQueryLinkedServer
AS
SELECT * FROM [MyLinkedserver].pubs.dbo.authors
```

but when you run this query from your application you get the following error:

Heterogeneous queries require the ANSI_NULLS and ANSI_WARNINGS options to be set for the connection. This ensures consistent query semantics. Enable these options and then reissue your query.

However when you test the SELECT statement in Query Analyzer it works fine. What do you need to do to fix this problem?

contributed by Edward Harling

Choose one of the answers below:

1. Modify your application's ODBC connection and check the "Use ANSI nulls, paddings and warnings" option.

2. Update the SQL Server Client Network Utility and check the "Automatic ANSI to OEM conversion" and "Use international settings" options.

3. Modify the code as follows:

```
CREATE PROCEDURE dbo.spQueryLinkedServer
AS
SET ANSI_NULLS ON
SELECT * FROM
[MyLinkedserver].pubs.dbo.authors
```

4. Modify the code as follows:

```
SET ANSI_NULLS ON
GO
CREATE PROCEDURE dbo.spQueryLinkedServer
AS
 SELECT * FROM
 [MyLinkedserver].pubs.dbo.authors
```

Answer:

4. Modify the code as follows:

```
SET ANSI_NULLS ON
GO
CREATE PROCEDURE dbo.spQueryLinkedServer
AS
 SELECT * FROM
 [MyLinkedserver].pubs.dbo.authors
```

SQL Server 2000 Enterprise Manager sets ANSI_NULLS to off by Default, so you must explicitly set it to ON in the stored procedure dialog box.

See the Microsoft Knowledge Base Article 296769 at, http://support.microsoft.com/default.aspx?scid=kb;en-us;296769 for more information.

Question 87 - T-SQL

There is the data in the People table:

```
foo_id      name      age
----------- --------- -----------
1           Foo       20
2           Bar       19
3           Hello     20
4           World     20
```

How many rows from the People table will be returned by the following query?

```
SELECT TOP 1 WITH TIES *
FROM People
ORDER BY age DESC
```

Contributed by Marek Grzenkowicz

Choose one of the answers below:

1. Instead of data from the table, this will return the dependencies on the table.
2. 1 row
3. 3 rows
4. The query will not execute, because there is a syntax error in it.

Answer:

3. 3 rows

3 rows will be returned. WITH TIES option used in SELECT clause specifies that additional rows be returned from the base result set with the same value in the ORDER BY columns appearing as the last of the TOP n (PERCENT) rows. TOP ... WITH TIES can only be specified if an ORDER BY clause is specified.

Question 88 - T-SQL

You have the following data and query:

```
    Tab_A        Tab_B

Id_A  Ds_A    Id_B Ds_B
----  -----   ---- ----
  1   A1      2     B1
  2   A2      3     B2
  3   A3      4     B3
```

```
Select Id_A,Id_B,Ds_A,Ds_B
 from Tab_A
   Join Tab_B
     On Id_A = Id_B
```

Which of the following queries returns the same results as the query above?

contributed by Necrossomus

Choose one of the answers below:

1.

```
Select Id_A,Id_B,Ds_A,Ds_B
  From Tab_A
    Cross Join Tab_B
```

2.

```
Select Id_A,Id_B,Ds_A,Ds_B
  From Tab_A
    Left Join Tab_B
      On Id_A = Id_B
```

3.

```
Select Id_A,Id_B,Ds_A,Ds_B
  From Tab_A
    Right Join Tab_B
      On Id_A = Id_B
```

4.

```
Select Id_A,Id_B,Ds_A,Ds_B
 From Tab_A
   Middle Join Tab_B
```

```
On Id_A = Id_B
```

Answer:

4.

```
Select Id_A,Id_B,Ds_A,Ds_B
 From Tab_A
   Middle Join Tab_B
    On Id_A = Id_B
```

The MIDDLE JOIN and JOIN keywords return the same values, but MIDDLE is not a valid keyword. The parser treats MIDDLE as an alias for the table. A right outer join returns non matching rows from the table on the right side of the join clause. A left join returns nonmatching rows on the left side of the join clause. Both of these do include the matching rows as well. A cross join returns all combinations of the rows from the two tables. The middle join acts like an inner join, which is the default when just specifying join. It is the same as specifying

```
Select Id_A,Id_B,Ds_A,Ds_B
 From Tab_A Middle
   Join Tab_B B
    On Middle.Id_A = B.Id_B
```

Question 89 - T-SQL

In SQL Server 2000, which of the below statements will give syntax error while creating respective tables? (Hint: Observe the syntax) --Plz. do not run the script before answering

```
1)
CREATE TABLE test111
( Fname varchar(30) NOT NULL,
  Lname varchar(30) NOT NULL,
  Compname varchar(30) NULL,
)
2)
CREATE TABLE test222
( fname varchar(30) NOT NULL,
  lname varchar(30) NOT NULL,
  compname varchar(30) NULL)
```

Choose one of the answers below:

1. 1
2. 2
3. Neither
4. Both

Answer:

3. Neither
Both statements will create tables irrespective of the COMMA in the last column of the first CREATE TABLE statement. This may be a bug in SQL Server, although the specific syntax in BOL does not specify that a comma cannot follow the final column.

Question 90 - T-SQL

Which of the following is an example of a DCL command, a DDL command, and a DML command?
contributed by Necrossomus

Choose one of the answers below:

1. SELECT, GRANT, DELETE
2. GRANT, CREATE, DENY
3. DELETE, UPDATE, INSERT
4. CREATE, GRANT, DENY
5. DENY, DROP, UPDATE

Answer:

5. DENY, DROP, UPDATE
Answer 5 (E) is correct. DCL statements control access to information (GRANT, DENT, REVOKE). DDL statements define SQL objects (CREATE, DROP) and DML statements manipulate the data (SELECT, INSERT, UPDATE, DELETE)

Question 91 - T-SQL

```
Create table DemoTab1
(
  clientno integer,
  dob datetime
)
go
insert into DemoTab1 values(1,getdate())
insert into DemoTab1 values(2,null)
go
select clientno, isnull(dob,+2) as DOB from DemoTab1
```

What is the output of the select statement for the row with clientno 2?

contributed by Vinod Devasia

Choose one of the answers below:

1. The current date.
2. 1900-01-03 00:00:00.000
3. 1900-01-01 00:00:00.000
4. +2

Answer:

2. 1900-01-03 00:00:00.000
The null value in SQL Server is converted to 1/1/1900 automatically by the server. SQL Server then adds 2 days to the this value for the datetime, which has been changed to 1900-01-01 00:00:00.000. The result is 1/3/1900.

Question 92 - T-SQL

What will the follwoing SQL statement return IN SQL Server 2000?

```
select convert(varchar(2), 1000000)
```

Choose one of the answers below:

1. 10
2. An Overflow Error
3. *
4. 0

Answer:

3. *

This returns a "*". From BOL: When converting character or binary expressions (char, varchar, binary, or varbinary) to an expression of a different data type, data can be truncated, only partially displayed, or an error is returned because the result is too short to display. Conversions to char, varchar, nchar, nvarchar, binary, and varbinary are truncated, except for the conversions shown in this table." This truncation returns a "*" in the conversions from integer based values to char, varchar, or the Unicode equivalents.

Question 93 - T-SQL

This code works:

```
declare @tmp numeric(38,4)
set @tmp = 9999999999 * 11
select @tmp
```

This code works:

```
declare @tmp numeric(38,4)
set @tmp = 99999999 * 11
select @tmp
```

What does this return?

```
declare @tmp numeric(38,4)
set @tmp = 999999999 * 11
select @tmp
```

Choose one of the answers below:

1. 109999999989.0000
2. 10999999999989.0000
3. 1099999999989.0000
4. An arithmetic overflow error

Answer:

4. An arithmetic overflow error

This code returns an arithmetic overflow. Why? The first code contains 10 9s, which makes it just over 9 Billion. To store 9 Billion, you need a bigint type. The second code contains 8 9s, which is in the millions and can be stored in an int. the third code contains 9 9s and this can be stored in an int value. To perform the operation, SQL Server attempts to store the values in the same type of datatype. However, when the 9 9s are multiplied out, the implicit conversion to int no longer fits and causes an error. This is a place where the parser's rules of operations cause issues. The best guess is the big int conversion rules are lower in precendence to int conversion rules.

Question 95 - T-SQL

Look at those two SQL batches:

```
IF 0 = 1
  SET QUOTED_IDENTIFIER ON

SELECT TOP 1 * FROM "sysobjects"
GO
IF 0 = 1
  SET QUOTED_IDENTIFIER OFF

SELECT TOP 1 * FROM "sysobjects"
GO
```

Which of these scripts will execute?

Choose one of the answers below:

1. The scripts are identical, since the IF...ELSE statement block is never reached - both scripts will execute.
2. The scripts are identical, since the IF...ELSE statement block is never reached - none of the scripts will execute.
3. Only script 1 will execute, because SET QUOTED_IDENTIFIER is set at parse time.
4. Only script 2 will execute, because SET QUOTED_IDENTIFIER is set at parse time.

Answer:

3. Only script 1 will execute, because SET QUOTED_IDENTIFIER is set at parse time.
Answer 3 (c) is correct. SET QUOTED_IDENTIFIER is set at parse time. Setting at parse time means that if the SET statement is present in the batch or stored procedure, it takes effect, regardless of whether code execution actually reaches that point; and the SET statement takes effect before any statements are executed.

Ref: SET QUOTED_IDENTIFIER - http://msdn.microsoft.com/library/default.asp?url=/library/en-us/tsqlref/ts_set-set_9jxu.asp.

Question 96 - T-SQL

Which of the following contains only DDL commaands?
contributed by Necrossomus

Choose one of the answers below:

1. SELECT, DELETE
2. GRANT,DENY
3. UPDATE, INSERT
4. CREATE, DROP, ALTER
5. DROP, UPDATE

Answer:

4. CREATE, DROP, ALTER
DDL commands are those that define SQL objects. Only answer 4 (D) contains just DDL commands. SELECT, UPDATE, INSERT, DELETE are DML commands and GRANT, REVOKE, DENY are DCL commands.

Question 97 - T-SQL

```
create table one ( col1 integer null)
go
insert into one values(1)
insert into one values(2)
insert into one values(3)
insert into one values(null)
go
create table two (  col1 integer null,  col2 integer
null)
go
insert into two values(1,1)
insert into two values(2,1)
insert into two values(3,1)
insert into two values(null,1)
go
select count(*) from one
select count(*) from two
```

What will the queries return?

contributed by Vinod Devasia

Choose one of the answers below:

1. 3 and 4.
2. 4 and 3.
3. Both return 4.
4. Both return 3

Answer:

3. Both return 4.
Test the code, to see the effect. From BOL : count() counts the total number of rows that meet the qualifications of the query. COUNT(*) returns the number of rows that match the search conditions specified in the query without eliminating duplicates. It counts each row separately, including rows that contain null values.

Question 98 - Tools

After copying selected tables in the Enterprise Manager Console window you paste the results into a text editor. What is the output that is pasted into the text editor?

Submitted by Brian Clarke

Choose one of the answers below:

1. The table names, table owners, table types and creation dates for each table

2. Create table statements for each table

3. Drop table and Create table statements for each table

4. General, Security and Dfs properties for each table

5. The column names and data for each table

Answer:

2. Create table statements for each table
Enterprise Manager will generate the create table statements for each table that you select by default. This does not appear to be documented anywhere, but it works if you try it.

Question 99 - Tools

In SQL Server 2000 Profiler, the numeric value given in the CPU column represents which of the following?

Choose one of the answers below:

1. Total percentage of CPU Utilization consumed by the event.
2. Average percentage of CPU utilization consumed by the event.
3. Total CPU time in milliseconds used by the event.
4. Total number of CPU cycles used by the event.

Answer:

3. Total CPU time in milliseconds used by the event.
The Correct answer is "Total CPU time in milliseconds used by the event". According to BOL under the section titled "SQL Profiler Data Columns", the CPU Heading which is selected by default when Profiler is opened is the amount of CPU time (in milliseconds) used by the event.

Question 100 - Tools

If you wish to add a template to the Query Analyzer templates list in the Object Browser, how do you do it? (assume the defaults have not been changed in Query Analyzer)

Choose one of the answers below:

1. Save them as .sql files in the "default installation\Microsoft SQL Server\80\Tools\Templates\SQL Query Analyzer" folder.
2. You cannot add templates to Query Analyzer, submit them to Microsoft to have them added in a Service Pack.
3. Save them as .tql files in your My Documents folder.
4. Save them as .tql files in the "default installation\Microsoft SQL Server\80\Tools\Templates\SQL Query Analyzer" folder.

Answer:

4. Save them as .tql files in the "default installation\Microsoft SQL Server\80\Tools\Templates\SQL Query Analyzer" folder.
The list of templates and template folders is read from the folder "SQL Query Analyzer", which by default is stored in c:\program files\Microsoft SQL Server\80\Tools\Templates folder. Under Tools Options, on the General tab in Query Analyzer you can change the Template folder as well as the extension that is used. Note, however, if you change the extension you will loose the Microsoft provided templates unless you change their extension to match or if you change the directory you will need to move the templates to either the top level of the defined location or no more than one subfolder below.

Ref: Query Analyzer Tricks -
http://www.sqlservercentral.com/columnists/sjones/queryanalyzertricks.asp
Using Templates in Query Analyzer -
http://msdn.microsoft.com/library/default.asp?url=/library/en-us/qryanlzr/qryanlzr_1dte.asp

---